HISTAMINE INTOLERANCE DIET

40+ Soup, Pizza, and Side Dishes recipes designed for Histamine Intolerance diet

TABLE OF CONTENTS

This document is geared towards providing exact and reliable information in regards to the topic and issue covered. The publication is sold with the idea that the publisher is not required to render accounting, officially permitted, or otherwise, qualified services. If advice is necessary, legal or professional, a practiced individual in the profession should be ordered.

Introduction

Histamine Intolerance recipes for personal enjoyment but also for family enjoyment. You will love them for sure for how easy it is to prepare them.

ZUCCHINI SOUP

Serves: **4**

Prep Time: **10**   Minutes

Cook Time: **20**   Minutes

Total Time: **30**   Minutes

INGREDIENTS

- 1 tablespoon olive oil
- 1 lb. zucchini
- ¼ red onion
- ½ cup all-purpose flour
- ¼ tsp salt
- ¼ tsp pepper
- 1 can vegetable broth
- 1 cup heavy cream

DIRECTIONS

1. In a saucepan heat olive oil and sauté zucchini until tender
2. Add remaining ingredients to the saucepan and bring to a boil

3. When all the vegetables are tender transfer to a blender and blend until smooth
4. Pour soup into bowls, garnish with parsley and serve

CUCUMBER SOUP

Serves: *2*
Prep Time: *10*   Minutes

Cook Time: *20*   Minutes

Total Time: *30*   Minutes

INGREDIENTS

- 2 tablespoons olive oil
- 2 cloves garlic
- ¼ cup lemon juice
- ¼ cup parsley
- ¼. cup cilantro
- ¼ cup greens
- 1 cup baby spinach
- 2 cups cucumber
- Salt
- radishes

DIRECTIONS

1. In a blender add all ingredients and blend until smooth
2. Season and refrigerate the soup
3. When ready pour soup into bowl and serve

VEGETARIAN MINESTRONE SOUP

Serves: 5

Prep Time: **10**   Minutes

Cook Time: **40**   Minutes

Total Time: **50**   Minutes

INGREDIENTS

- 1 tablespoon olive oil
- ¾ cup onion
- 2 ½ cups water
- 2 cups zucchini
- 1 cup sliced carrots
- 1 cup beans
- ¼ cup celery
- 2 tablespoons basil
- 1/3 tsp oregano
- ¼ tsp black pepper
- 1 can plum tomatoes
- 2 cloves garlic
- ½ cup uncooked pasta

DIRECTIONS

1. **In a saucepan add oil, onion and sauté for 4-5 minutes**

2. Add remaining ingredients and bring to a boil
3. Reduce heat and simmer on low heat for 20-25 minutes
4. Add pasta and cook until pasta is al dente for 10-12 minutes
5. When ready, remove from heat and serve

CABBAGE STEW

Serves: *4*
Prep Time: *10*   Minutes

Cook Time: *40*   Minutes

Total Time: *50*   Minutes

INGREDIENTS

- 1 lb. bison
- 1 tablespoon olive oil
- ¼ cabbage
- 2 carrots
- 1 onion
- 2 cloves garlic
- 2 tablespoons aminos
- 4 cups chicken stock

DIRECTIONS

1. In a pot sauté the carrot, onion and cabbage for 2-3 minutes
2. Add bison and cook for 4-5 minutes
3. Add chicken stock, garlic, ginger and coconut aminos
4. Cook for 25-30 minutes
5. When ready from heat garnish with pepper and serve

CHICKEN RICE SOUP

Serves: **4**

Prep Time: **10**   Minutes

Cook Time: **40**   Minutes

Total Time: **50**   Minutes

INGREDIENTS

- 1 tablespoon olive oil
- 1 cup carrot
- 1 cup onion
- 1 cup celery
- 1 chicken breast
- 2 cloves garlic
- 6 cups chicken broth
- ½ cup brown rice
- ¼ cup lemon juice
- 1 tsp black pepper
- ¼ cup parsley

DIRECTIONS

1. In a pot sauté the carrot, onion and celery for 2-3 minutes
2. Add chicken breast and cook for another 4-5 minutes
3. Add rice, lemon juice, pepper and chicken broth

4. Cook for 30-40 minutes on high heat
5. When soup is cooked remove from heat
6. Garnish with parsley and serve

MISO SOUP

Serves: **2**
Prep Time: **10** Minutes

Cook Time: **20** Minutes

Total Time: **30** Minutes

INGREDIENTS

- 2 tablespoons arame
- 1 cup water
- 2 cups chicken broth
- 1 cup mushrooms
- 2 tablespoons miso paste
- 10 oz. codfish fillet
- 2 cups vegetables
- ¼ cup broccoli sprouts
- 1 tablespoon scallion
- 1 tablespoon olive oil

DIRECTIONS

1. In a bowl soak arame and set aside
2. In a saucepan add broth and bring to a boil
3. Add the cod to the saucepan, vegetables. cover and cook for 5-6 minutes
4. Stir in the miso paste and cook until soup is ready

5. Ladle into bowls top with scallions and serve

MUSHROOM SOUP

Serves: **6**

Prep Time: **20** Minutes

Cook Time: **35** Minutes

Total Time: **55** Minutes

INGREDIENTS

- 2 tablespoons olive oil
- 2 onions
- 2 celery sticks
- 4 garlic cloves
- 4 sprigs of rosemary
- 3 carrots
- 3 cups mushrooms
- 4 cups vegetable broth
- 2 bay leaves

DIRECTIONS

1. In a saucepan sauté garlic, celery, onions until soft
2. Add mushrooms, carrots and sauté for another 4-5 minutes
3. Add bay leaves, broth and simmer for 25-30 minutes
4. When ready remove from heat and serve

CHICKEN SOUP

Serves: **4**

Prep Time: **15**   Minutes

Cook Time: **50**   Minutes

Total Time: **65**   Minutes

INGREDIENTS

- 1 chicken
- 2 tablespoons coconut oil
- 2 l water
- 2 tablespoons apple cider vinegar
- 2 onions
- 6 carrots
- 5 celery sticks
- 2 zucchinis
- 1-inch ginger root
- 4 cloves garlic
- 1 bunch parsley

DIRECTIONS

1. Cut chicken into pieces and place in a pot
2. Add water, vinegar, parsley and boil for 50-60 minutes
3. Meanwhile add the rest of the ingredients

4. Simmer for 5-6 hours on low heat

5. When ready remove from heat and serve

ASPARAGUS SOUP

Serves: *4*

Prep Time: *10*   Minutes

Cook Time: *50*   Minutes

Total Time: *60*   Minutes

INGREDIENTS

- 8 oz. fennel bulbs
- 10 oz. asparagus
- 1 bunch onions
- 3 cups water
- 1 tsp salt
- 2 tablespoons rice
- 2 leeks
- 2 tablespoons sesame oil
- ¼ cup dill
- ¼ cup mint leaves
- 2 cups vegetable broth
- 2 tablespoons lemon juice

DIRECTIONS

1. In a skillet heat olive oil and sauté onion, dill and mint leaves
2. Slice the vegetables and place them in a pot

3. Add salt, rice, water and simmer for 35-45 minutes
4. Add sautéed ingredients to the soup and simmer for another 4-5 minutes
5. When ready blend the soup and serve

SEASWEED SOUP

Serves: 2
Prep Time: 15 Minutes

Cook Time: 20 Minutes

Total Time: 35 Minutes

INGREDIENTS

- 2 cups water
- 1 tablespoon soy sauce
- 2 oz. seaweed
- ¼ cup tofu
- 1-inch ginger
- 1 tsp olive oil
- 2 garlic cloves
- 4 scallions

DIRECTIONS

1. In a soup pot add water, scallion, ginger, garlic and bring to a boil
2. In a skillet heat olive oil and sauté tofu
3. Add sautéed tofu to the soup and the rest of the ingredients
4. Cook until soup is cooked
5. When ready remove from heat garnish with scallions and serve

SIDE DISHES

SESAME PORK TACOS

Serves: **4**

Prep Time: **5**   Minutes

Cook Time: **15**   Minutes

Total Time: **25**   Minutes

INGREDIENTS

- 1 cup cucumber slices
- 5 radishes
- ½ cup red wine vinegar
- 3 tsp sugar
- 1 tablespoon olive oil
- 3 scallions
- 1 cup red cabbage
- 1 lb. ground pork
- 2 tsp garlic powder
- 2 tablespoons sesame oil
- 2 tablespoons soy sauce
- 1 tsp Sriracha
- 10 tortillas
- 1 tsp cilantro
- ¼ cup sour cream

DIRECTIONS

1. In a bowl add radishes, cucumbers, vinegar, 1 tsp sugar and salt, stir well to combine

2. In a pan add oil, scallions, cabbage and cook for 4-5 minutes

3. Add pork, sugar, garlic powder and cook for another 4-5 minutes

4. Add soy sauce, sesame oil and stir to combine

5. Spread sour cream in the center of your tortilla, add pork filling and sprinkle cilantro, radishes and top with meat mixture

WATERMELON GAZPACHO

Serves: *3*
Prep Time: *10* Minutes

Cook Time: *10* Minutes

Total Time: *20* Minutes

INGREDIENTS

- 2 cups ripe watermelon
- 1 red pepper
- ¼ onion
- 3 tablespoons red wine vinegar
- 6 tablespoons cranberry juice
- Italian basil leaves as needed

DIRECTIONS

1. Puree all ingredients, except the basil, until smooth
2. Refrigerate to chill
3. Serve garnished with basil, onion, tomato or cucumber

LIME GRILLED CORN

Serves: **3**
Prep Time: **5**   Minutes

Cook Time: **15**   Minutes

Total Time: **20**   Minutes

INGREDIENTS

- 3 ears of corn
- 2 tablespoons mayonnaise
- 2 tablespoons squeezed lime juice
- ½ tsp chili powder
- 1 pinch of salt

DIRECTIONS

1. Place corn onto the grill and cook for 5-6 minutes or until the kernels being to brown
2. Turn every few minutes until all sides are slightly charred
3. In a bowl mix the rest of ingredients
4. Spread a light coating of the mixture onto each cob and serve

MACADAMIA DIP WITH VEGETABLES

Serves: **4**

Prep Time: **10**   Minutes

Cook Time: **30**   Minutes

Total Time: **40**   Minutes

INGREDIENTS

- 6 oz. squash
- ½ bunch basil
- ¼ cup macadamia nuts
- 1 tablespoon olive oil
- ¼ lemon
- ¼ tsp ground smoked paprika
- salt
- vegetable sticks

DIRECTIONS

1. Preheat the oven to 350 F
2. Cut the squash into chunks and roast for 25-30 minutes
3. In a food processor add the basil leaves, lemon zest, macadamia nuts, squash pieces and salt
4. Serve with vegetable sticks: cucumber, carrots, tomatoes and green pepper

GINGERSNAPS

Serves: *6*

Prep Time: *10* Minutes

Cook Time: *15* Minutes

Total Time: *25* Minutes

INGREDIENTS

- 1 cup white whole wheat flour
- 1 cornstarch
- 1 tsp baking powder
- 1 tsp ground ginger
- ½ tsp ground cinnamon
- ¼ tsp nutmeg
- ¼ tsp ground cloves
- 1 tablespoon unsalted butter
- 1 egg white
- 2 tsp vanilla stevia
- ½ cup nonfat milk
- ½ cup molasses
- 1 tsp vanilla extract

DIRECTIONS

1. Preheat the oven to 350 F

2. In a bowl whisk together the cornstarch, ginger, baking powder, cinnamon, nutmeg, cloves and salt and flour

3. In another bowl mix vanilla extract, egg, butter, stevia, molasses and milk

4. Add in the flour mixture and stir until fully incorporated

5. Divide dough into 14-16 portions and roll each into a ball

6. Place onto a baking sheet and press it down into the cookie dough

7. Bake for 8-10 minutes

8. When ready, remove and serve

TURKEY & VEGGIES STUFFED PEPPERS

Serves: **4**

Prep Time: **10** Minutes

Cook Time: **40** Minutes

Total Time: **50** Minutes

INGREDIENTS

- 4 red bell peppers
- 1 lb. ground turkey
- 1 tablespoon olive oil
- ¼ onion
- 1 cup mushrooms 1 zucchini
- ½ green bell pepper
- ½ yellow bell pepper
- 1 cup spinach
- 1 can diced tomatoes
- 1 tsp Italian seasoning
- ¼ tsp garlic powder
- 1 pinch of salt

DIRECTIONS

1. Preheat the oven to 325 F
2. In a pot bring water to boil, add pepper and cook for 5-6 minutes

3. In a skillet cook the turkey until brown and set aside

4. In another pan add onion, olive oil, mushrooms, zucchini, green, yellow pepper, spinach and cook until tender

5. Add remaining ingredients to the turkey and cook until done

6. Stuff the peppers with the mixture and place them into a casserole dish

7. Bake for 15-18 minutes or until done

QUINOA TACO MEAT

Serves: *6*
Prep Time: *10*   Minutes

Cook Time: *50*   Minutes

Total Time: *60*   Minutes

INGREDIENTS

- 1 cup red quinoa
- 1 cup vegetable broth
- ¾ cup water

SEASONING

- ¼ cup salsa
- 1 tablespoon yeast
- 1 tsp cumin
- 1 tsp chili powder
- ¼ tsp garlic powder
- ½ tsp black pepper
- ½ tsp salt
- 1 tablespoon olive oil

DIRECTIONS

1. In a saucepan add quinoa and cook for 5-6 minutes
2. Add water, vegetable broth and bring to a boil

3. Reduce heat to low and cook for 20-22 minutes or until liquid is absorbed

4. Add quinoa to a mixing bowl, remaining ingredients and toss to combine

5. Bake for 25-30 minutes or until golden brown

6. When ready remove and serve with taco salads, enchiladas or nachos

KALE CHIPS

Serves: *6*
Prep Time: *10* Minutes

Cook Time: *25* Minutes

Total Time: *35* Minutes

INGREDIENTS

- 1 bunch of kale
- 1 tablespoon olive oil
- 1 tsp salt

DIRECTIONS

1. Preheat the oven to 325 F
2. Chop the kale into chip size pieces
3. Put pieces into a bowl tops with olive oil and salt
4. Spread the leaves in a single layer onto a parchment paper
5. Bake for 20-25 minutes
6. When ready, remove and serve

CHICKEN AND BROWN RICE PASTA

Serves: 2

Prep Time: **10**   Minutes

Cook Time: **15**   Minutes

Total Time: **25**   Minutes

INGREDIENTS

- 1 cup cooked rice pasta
- 1 chicken breast
- ¼ cup no sugar marinara sauce
- ½ cup tomatoes
- parsley for serving
- 1 tsp olive oil

DIRECTIONS

1. In a skillet cook the pasta according to the package directions
2. Drain and rinse the pasta
3. Add cooked chicken breast, marinara sauce and serve

PHILLY CHEESE STEAK

Serves: **4**

Prep Time: **5**   Minutes

Cook Time: **20**   Minutes

Total Time: **25**   Minutes

INGREDIENTS

- 2 tsp olive oil
- 1 onion
- 3 portobello mushrooms
- 1 red bell pepper
- 1 tsp dried oregano
- ¼ tsp ground pepper
- 1 tablespoon all-purpose flour
- ½ cup vegetable broth
- 1 tablespoon soy sauce
- 2 oz. vegan cheese
- 3 whole-wheat rolls

DIRECTIONS

1. In a skillet add onion, pepper, bell pepper, oregano and cook until soft
2. Reduce heat, sprinkle flour, soy sauce, broth and bring to a simmer

3. Remove from heat, add cheese slices on top and let it stand until fully melted
4. Divide into 3-4 portions and serve

CAULIFLOWER WINGS

Serves: *4*

Prep Time: *10*   Minutes

Cook Time: *50*   Minutes

Total Time: *60*   Minutes

INGREDIENTS

- 1 head cauliflower
- ¼ unsweetened almond milk
- ¼ cup water
- ¾ rice flour
- 1 tsp garlic powder
- 1 tsp onion powder
- 1 tsp cumin
- 1 tsp paprika
- ½ tsp salt
- ¼ tsp ground pepper
- bbq sauce

VINEGAR SAUCE
- 1 tablespoon vegan butter
- 2 tablespoons apple cider vinegar
- 1 tablespoon water
- 1 pinch of salt

37

DIRECTIONS

1. Preheat the oven to 425 F

2. Mix all wing ingredients in a bowl and submerge each cauliflower floret into the mix

3. Place florets on a prepare baking sheet

4. Bake for 10 minutes, flip and bake for another 10 minutes or until golden brown

5. Remove the cauliflower from the oven and serve with vinegar sauce

6. When ready season with pepper and salt and serve

ROASTED BOK CHOY

Serves: **4**

Prep Time: **5**   Minutes

Cook Time: **15**   Minutes

Total Time: **20**   Minutes

INGREDIENTS

- 5 heads baby bok choy
- olive oil
- 1 tsp pepper
- 1 tsp salt

DIRECTIONS

1. Preheat the oven to 425 F
2. Cut each bok choy in half lengthwise and place on a baking sheet
3. Drizzle with olive oil, pepper and salt
4. Bake for 10-12 minutes, flip and bake for another 8-10 minutes
5. When ready remove and serve

GREEN PESTO PASTA

Serves: 2

Prep Time: 5   Minutes

Cook Time: 15   Minutes

Total Time: 20   Minutes

INGREDIENTS

- 4 oz. spaghetti
- 2 cups basil leaves
- 2 garlic cloves
- ¼ cup olive oil
- 2 tablespoons parmesan cheese
- ½ tsp black pepper

DIRECTIONS

1. Bring water to a boil and add pasta
2. In a blend add parmesan cheese, basil leaves, garlic and blend
3. Add olive oil, pepper and blend again
4. Pour pesto onto pasta and serve when ready

TACO SALAD

Serves: **2**

Prep Time: **5**   Minutes

Cook Time: **5**   Minutes

Total Time: **10** Minutes

INGREDIENTS

- ½ cup olive oil
- 1 lb. cooked steak
- 1 tablespoon taco seasoning
- Juice of 1 lime
- 1 tsp cumin
- 1 head romaine lettuce
- 1 cup corn
- 1 cup beans
- 1 cup tomatoes

DIRECTIONS

1. In a bowl mix all ingredients and mix well
2. Serve with dressing

KALE SALAD

Serves: **2**

Prep Time: **5**   Minutes

Cook Time: **5**   Minutes

Total Time: **10**   Minutes

INGREDIENTS

- 2 cups kale
- 1 tablespoon hemp seeds
- 1 cucumber
- 1 tsp honey
- 1 tsp olive oil
- 1 handful parsley

DIRECTIONS

1. In a bowl mix all ingredients and mix well
2. Serve with dressing

ROASTED LOW HISTAMNE SALAD

Serves: **2**
Prep Time: **5**   Minutes

Cook Time: **5**   Minutes

Total Time: **10**   Minutes

INGREDIENTS

- 1 cup cauliflower
- 1 cup broccoli
- 1 cup brussels sprouts
- 1 cup red bell pepper
- 1 cup squash
- 1 tablespoon olive oil

DIRECTIONS

1. In a bowl mix all ingredients and mix well
2. Serve with dressing

PUMPKIN SALAD

Serves: **2**
Prep Time: **5**   Minutes
Cook Time: **5**   Minutes
Total Time: **10** Minutes

INGREDIENTS

- ½ cauliflower florets
- 1 cup pumpkin
- 1 cup Brussel sprouts
- 1 cup quinoa
- 1 tablespoon olive oil

DIRECTIONS

1. In a bowl mix all ingredients and mix well
2. Serve with dressing

RED CHICORY SALAD

Serves: **2**

Prep Time: **5** Minutes

Cook Time: **5** Minutes

Total Time: **10** Minutes

INGREDIENTS

- 2 red chicory
- 2 fennel bulbs
- ½ cup watercress
- 2 garlic cloves
- 1 tablespoon olive oil

DIRECTIONS

1. In a bowl mix all ingredients and mix well
2. Serve with dressing

FENNEL SALAD

Serves: **2**
Prep Time: **5**   Minutes

Cook Time: **5**   Minutes

Total Time: **10** Minutes

INGREDIENTS

- 1 fennel bulb
- 1 tablespoon lemon juice
- ¼ cup olive oil
- 1 tsp mint
- 1 tsp onion

DIRECTIONS

1. In a bowl mix all ingredients and mix well
2. Serve with dressing

GIGNER CILANTRO SALAD

Serves: *2*
Prep Time: *5*   Minutes

Cook Time: *5*   Minutes

Total Time: *10* Minutes

INGREDIENTS

- 2 lb. sweet potatoes
- ¼ cup olive oil
- 2 tablespoons lemon juice
- ¼ cup scallions
- ¼ cup cilantro
- ¼ tsp salt

DIRECTIONS

1. In a bowl mix all ingredients and mix well
2. Serve with dressing

WATERCRESS FRITATTA

Serves: **2**

Prep Time: **10** Minutes

Cook Time: **20** Minutes

Total Time: **30** Minutes

INGREDIENTS

- ½ lb. watercress
- 1 tablespoon olive oil
- ½ red onion
- ¼ tsp salt
- 2 oz. cheddar cheese
- 1 garlic clove
- ¼ tsp dill

DIRECTIONS

1. In a bowl whisk eggs with salt and cheese
2. In a frying pan heat olive oil and pour egg mixture
3. Add remaining ingredients and mix well
4. Serve when ready

KALE FRITATTA

Serves: *2*
Prep Time: *10* Minutes

Cook Time: *20* Minutes

Total Time: *30* Minutes

INGREDIENTS

- 1 cup kale
- 1 tablespoon olive oil
- ½ red onion
- ¼ tsp salt
- 2 oz. cheddar cheese
- 1 garlic clove
- ¼ tsp dill

DIRECTIONS

1. In a skillet sauté kale until tender
2. In a bowl whisk eggs with salt and cheese
3. In a frying pan heat olive oil and pour egg mixture
4. Add remaining ingredients and mix well
5. When ready serve with sautéed kale

MEDITERRANENA BUDDA BOWL

Serves: **1**

Prep Time: **10** Minutes

Cook Time: **10** Minutes

Total Time: **20** Minutes

INGREDIENTS

- 1 zucchini
- ¼ tsp oregano
- Salt
- 1 cup cooked quinoa
- 1 cup spinach
- 1 cup mixed greens
- ½ cup red pepper
- ¼ cup cucumber
- ¼ cup tomatoes
- parsley
- tahini dressing

DIRECTIONS

1. In a skillet heat olive oil olive and sauté zucchini until soft and sprinkle oregano over zucchini

2. In a bowl add the rest of ingredients and toss to combine
3. Add fried zucchini and mix well
4. Pour over tahini dressing, mix well and serve

VEGAN CURRY

Serves: *4*
Prep Time: *10*   Minutes

Cook Time: *20*   Minutes

Total Time: *30*   Minutes

INGREDIENTS

- 1 tablespoon olive oil
- ¼ cup onion
- 2 stalks celery
- 1 garlic clove
- ¼ tsp coriander
- ¼ tsp cumin
- ¼ tsp turmeric
- ¼ tsp red pepper flakes
- 1 cauliflower
- 1 zucchini
- 2 tomatoes
- 1 tsp salt
- 1 cup vegetable broth
- 1 handful of baby spinach
- 1 tablespoon almonds
- 1 tablespoon cilantro

DIRECTIONS

1. In a skillet heat olive oil and sauté celery, garlic and onions for 4-5 minutes or until vegetables are tender

2. Add cumin, spices, coriander, cumin, turmeric red pepper flakes stir to combine and cook for another 1-2 minutes

3. Add zucchini, cauliflower, tomatoes, broth, spinach, water and simmer on low heat for 15-20 minutes

4. Add remaining ingredients and simmer for another 4-5 minutes

5. Garnish curry and serve

CAULIFLOWER WITH ROSEMARY

Serves: **2**
Prep Time: **5**   Minutes

Cook Time: **15**   Minutes

Total Time: **20**   Minutes

INGREDIENTS

- 1 cauliflower
- 1 tablespoon rosemary
- 1 cup vegetable stock
- 2 garlic cloves
- salt

DIRECTIONS

1. In a saucepan add cauliflower, stock and bring to a boil for 12-15 minutes
2. Blend cauliflower until smooth, add garlic, salt, rosemary and blend again
3. When ready pour in a bowl and serve

BRUSSELS SPROUTS

Serves: **2**

Prep Time: **10** Minutes

Cook Time: **20** Minutes

Total Time: **30** Minutes

INGREDIENTS

- 1 tablespoon olive oil
- 2 shallots
- 2 cloves garlic
- 1 lb. brussels sprouts
- 1 cup vegetable stock
- 4 springs thyme
- ¼ cup pine nuts

DIRECTIONS

1. In a pan heat olive oil and cook shallots until tender
2. Add garlic, sprouts, thyme, stock and cook for another 4-5 minutes
3. Cover and cook for another 10-12 minutes or until sprouts are soft
4. When ready add pine nuts and serve

PIZZA

SIMPLE PIZZA RECIPE

Serves: **6-8**
Prep Time: **10** Minutes

Cook Time: **15** Minutes

Total Time: **25** Minutes

INGREDIENTS

- 1 pizza crust
- ½ cup tomato sauce
- ¼ black pepper
- 1 cup pepperoni slices
- 1 cup mozzarella cheese
- 1 cup olives

DIRECTIONS

1. Spread tomato sauce on the pizza crust
2. Place all the toppings on the pizza crust
3. Bake the pizza at 425 F for 12-15 minutes
4. When ready remove pizza from the oven and serve

ZUCCHINI PIZZA

Serves: **6-8**

Prep Time: **10** Minutes

Cook Time: **15** Minutes

Total Time: **25** Minutes

INGREDIENTS

- 1 pizza crust
- ½ cup tomato sauce
- ¼ black pepper
- 1 cup zucchini slices
- 1 cup mozzarella cheese
- 1 cup olives

DIRECTIONS

1. Spread tomato sauce on the pizza crust
2. Place all the toppings on the pizza crust
3. Bake the pizza at 425 F for 12-15 minutes
4. When ready remove pizza from the oven and serve

CAULIFLOWER RECIPE

Serves: **6-8**
Prep Time: **10**   Minutes

Cook Time: **15**   Minutes

Total Time: **25**   Minutes

INGREDIENTS

- 1 pizza crust
- ½ cup tomato sauce
- ¼ black pepper
- 1 cup cauliflower
- 1 cup mozzarella cheese
- 1 cup olives

DIRECTIONS

1. Spread tomato sauce on the pizza crust
2. Place all the toppings on the pizza crust
3. Bake the pizza at 425 F for 12-15 minutes
4. When ready remove pizza from the oven and serve

BROCCOLI RECIPE

Serves: **6-8**
Prep Time: **10**   Minutes

Cook Time: **15**   Minutes

Total Time: **25**   Minutes

INGREDIENTS

- 1 pizza crust
- ½ cup tomato sauce
- ¼ black pepper
- 1 cup broccoli
- 1 cup mozzarella cheese
- 1 cup olives

DIRECTIONS

1. Spread tomato sauce on the pizza crust
2. Place all the toppings on the pizza crust
3. Bake the pizza at 425 F for 12-15 minutes
4. When ready remove pizza from the oven and serve

TOMATOES & HAM PIZZA

Serves: **6-8**
Prep Time: **10**   Minutes
Cook Time: **15**   Minutes
Total Time: **25**   Minutes

INGREDIENTS

- 1 pizza crust
- ½ cup tomato sauce
- ¼ black pepper
- 1 cup pepperoni slices
- 1 cup tomatoes
- 6-8 ham slices
- 1 cup mozzarella cheese
- 1 cup olives

DIRECTIONS

1. Spread tomato sauce on the pizza crust
2. Place all the toppings on the pizza crust
3. Bake the pizza at 425 F for 12-15 minutes
4. When ready remove pizza from the oven and serve

THANK YOU FOR READING THIS BOOK!

CPSIA information can be obtained
at www.ICGtesting.com
Printed in the USA
BVHW031013150321
602551BV00004B/272